# IRISH DANCE TUNES FOR ALL HARPS

## 50 Jigs, Reels, Hornpipes, and Airs

# By SYLVIA WOODS

edited by SYLVIA WOODS and MAIRE NI CHATHASAIGH
with special introduction by Danny Carnahan

## DEDICATION

This book is lovingly dedicated to Dinny, the Barron family, and all the harpers in Buncrana, County Donegal, Ireland.

## MANY THANKS TO:

Maire ni Chathasaigh for all of her expertise and assistance, especially in the fine art of ornamenting Irish music.

And to Danny Carnahan for his informative introduction.

Cover art by Steve Duglas

All arrangements by Sylvia Woods

First printing 1984
Second printing 1987
Third printing 1996
2nd Edition  - re-typeset 2014

© 1984 and 2014 by Sylvia Woods
Sylvia Woods Harp Center, Woods Music & Books
PO Box 223434, Princeville HI 96722 USA
www.harpcenter.com

ISBN 978-0-9602990-4-1

# TABLE OF CONTENTS

Introduction - by Sylvia Woods...................ii
Irish Dance Tunes - by Danny Carnahan ...iv

JIGS

    Blarney Pilgrim.........................1
    Garryowen ..............................2
    Geese in the Bog.......................3
    Haste to the Wedding...................4
    Maid at the Spinning Wheel.............5
    Merrily Kiss the Quaker ...............6
    Money in Both Pockets .................7
    Morrison's Jig.........................8
    Off She Goes ..........................9
    Road to Lisdoonvarna...................10
    Smash the Windows.....................11
    Tobin's Favorites .....................12

SLIP JIGS

    A Fig for a Kiss ......................13
    Boys of Ballysodare ...................14
    Dublin Streets ........................15
    Give Us a Drink of Water...............16
    Hardiman the Fiddler...................17
    Kid on the Mountain....................18
    Rocky Road to Dublin...................20

HORNPIPES

    Boys of Blue Hill......................21
    Fisher's Hornpipe .....................22
    Ladies' Hornpipe ......................23
    Little Beggarman ......................24
    O'Donnell's Hornpipe ..................25

Off to California .....................26
Plains of Boyle .......................27
Rights of Man .........................28
Soldier's Joy .........................29

REELS

    Earl's Chair ..........................30
    Fairy Dance Reel ......................31
    Green Fields of America................32
    Leather Buttons........................33
    Maid Behind the Bar ...................34
    Mason's Apron..........................35
    Miss McLeod's Reel.....................36
    Music in the Glen .....................37
    Musical Priest.........................38
    Tent at the Fair.......................39
    Thro' the Field .......................40
    Waterfall..............................41
    Who Made Your Breeches? ...............42
    Wind that Shakes the Barley ...........43
    Wise Maid..............................44

AIRS, MARCHES, AND OTHER TUNES

    Battle of Aughrim .....................45
    Brian Boru's March ....................46
    Pig Town Fling ........................47
    Carrickfergus .........................48
    King of the Fairies ...................50
    March of the King of Laois.............52
    Parting Glass..........................53

More Harp Books of Celtic Music ........54
Additional Harp Music by Sylvia Woods..55
Alphabetical Index of Tunes.............56

# INTRODUCTION
## by Sylvia Woods

Welcome to the world of Irish dance tunes. If you already play this type of music, you know how much fun it can be. And if you are new to jigs and reels, you are in for a real treat. I have chosen 50 tunes for this collection. Some are well known by most Irish musicians, and some are a bit more rare. They are all written in the keys in which they are most often played.

I am very pleased to announce that one of the finest players of dance tunes on the harp, Maire ni Chathasaigh, provided a great deal of assistance in this endeavor. She advised me on different settings of the tunes, and provided many of the ornaments. I am very grateful for her help.

Here are a few suggestions to assist you in playing this lively music. Please be sure to also read Danny Carnahan's fine introduction to Irish music, starting on page iv.

## DIFFERENT VERSIONS

Many of the tunes in this book have different variations, or settings, played by traditional musicians. Don't be surprised if your friends play a slightly different version of the melody or the chords. This is common. When musicians get together, they often compare notes on their tunes, and try different settings. If you're playing with other musicians you'll probably want to adapt your settings to fit so that the group will sound together.

You will probably also run across different names for some of these tunes, as well as totally different tunes with the same names. This comes from geographic differences, and the fact that many musicians learn tunes without learning the "correct" name, and then make up their own title. These "incorrect" titles are then passed on to other musicians . . . and the confusion continues. As Breandan Breathnach mentions in his book Folk Music and Dances of Ireland, one tune, *The Perthshire Hunt*, has at least 60 names.

## ORNAMENTATION

Ornamentation is very important in traditional Irish dance music. These tunes are never played straight, but are always ornamented with grace notes and variations, giving them their recognizable Irish feel. The best way to learn about ornaments is to listen to lots of dance tunes played by various instruments. Since each instrument has different patterns that are easily playable, each has different variations of the same ornaments. It is very helpful for the harper to listen to dance tunes played on fiddles, uilleann (elbow) pipes and tin whistles (also called penny whistles). The ornaments used by these instruments are basic to most ornamentation.

Many ornaments in this book are written in grace notes. ♪ A grace note should not be nearly as loud as the note it is accompanying. The melody note should always sound the strongest.

## VARIATIONS

Usually a tune will have a phrase (long or short) which repeats several times. These phrases will generally be played differently each time using variations and ornaments. You must hear the tune and listen for the similarities and differences in the phrases.

An example of a short phrase like this is found in *Morrison's Jig*. The first, third, and fifth measures are all actually the same. The first measure is the basic phrase, and the 3rd and 5th measures are variations.

Another good example of this is *Brian Boru's March*. This popular harp tune has more variations than you can shake a stick at. Everyone plays it differently. In my version, I tried to use as many variations as possible so you could see some of the possibilities. Actually, in each section, the first 6 measures are basically the same, except that they alternate up or down a step. You can use this setting to get ideas of how you'd like to arrange your own version.

Some melodic ornaments include:

(a) filling in gaps between notes

(b) changing the direction of the notes

(c) changing the order of the notes

(d) leaving out notes.

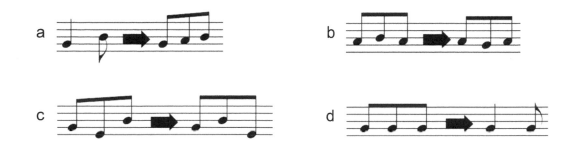

Ornaments must not throw your timing off. These are DANCE tunes, and the rhythm is of the utmost importance. If an ornament is ruining the flow of the rhythm, leave it out, or use a different ornament or variation.

Often the first line or phrase of a tune is played straight, with no ornaments. Then, each time a phrase is repeated, it is ornamented in a different fashion. These differences can be quite subtle, but they add to the overall pattern of the tune.

The arrangements in this book include ornaments, but they are only suggested possibilities. Experiment with various ornaments in different places to make the tune your own. Don't use the same ornaments on the repeats as you do during the first time through. Add variety to your settings by using ornaments and your tunes will sparkle with life.

**TUNES WITH NO ENDINGS**

As you are playing the tunes in this book, you will notice that some of them don't seem to end. They'll sound fine when you continue to repeat the sections of the tune, but there is no way to stop. This is because these dance tunes are often played in sets or medleys, one tune going directly into the next.

The best way to decide on how to end is just to let your ears and your rhythmic and melodic intuition tell you what to do. Often returning to the first chord of the piece will work, with a melody note in your right hand that is part of that chord. If what you try sounds logical and finished, it is probably correct.

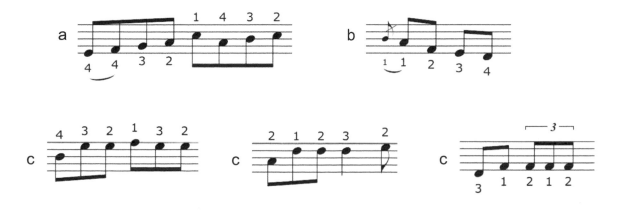

**FINGERINGS**

Some of the fingerings in this book may be unfamiliar to you, especially due to the ornamentation. Here are some of the unusual fingerings you will encounter.

    (a) sliding on the 4th finger
    (b) sliding the grace note with the thumb
    (c) various ways of changing fingers on the same note

# IRISH DANCE TUNES
## by Danny Carnahan

**WHAT ARE JIGS, REELS AND HORNPIPES?**

Jigs, reels and hornpipes are the three most common kinds of dance tunes played in Ireland. The number of beats per measure, the number of measures in a phrase, and the number of times through a tune were dictated by the steps and patterns of the dance. Nowadays, dance tunes are played as performance pieces as well as for dancers. This gives traditional musicians immense latitude in interpreting the tunes and choosing settings, tempos and medleys. But it doesn't hurt to know the older, conventional approaches, too.

Any musician who wishes to play Irish music should make a point of watching dancers dance the tunes. While I can explain much about tempos and rhythms here, the subtleties of the tunes as they lead the dancers through their moves can best be understood from live performances. Dancers can also give you an inkling of how and why the tunes evolved. This knowledge can give you a clearer idea of how the styles you prefer developed, and even perhaps where to take them next within the tradition.

**JIGS** (pages 1-12)

A jig is a tune in 6/8 time, most easily counted out like this: "ONE two three, four five six, ONE two three, four five six." When counting your way through, try not to give the "four" beat too much emphasis. If you do, the 6-beat measure breaks into a pair of 3-beat phrases, making the tune sound choppy. Jigs can be played comfortably as slow as ♩. = 100 or up to about ♩. =120.

**SLIP JIGS** (pages 13-20)

A slip-jig is in 9/8 time, like one-and-a-half jigs. Slip-jigs have been called jigs within jigs, because they consist of three groups of three beats in each measure. The way to count it is: "ONE two three, four five six, SEV'N eight nine, ONE two three, four five six, SEV'N eight nine." Give slightly less emphasis to the "SEV'N" as you do to the "ONE" down-beat. Tempos for slip-jigs are the same as for other jigs.

**REELS** (pages 30-44)

Reels are tunes in 4/4 time and are easily counted out: "ONE-and two-and, THREE-and four-and," with the downbeat getting the most emphasis. Comfortable tempos for reels range from ♩ = 92 to ♩ =112.

**HORNPIPES** (pages 21-29)

Hornpipes also have 4 beats in each measure. The rhythm of a hornpipe is more deliberate than a reel, with more emphasis on the third beat, and is given a strong loping gait by using slightly dotted rhythms. In a hornpipe, each beat is divided up into one long and one short note: ♪. ♪ Count it out: "ONE-and two-and, THREE-and four and," with very short "ands" and with nearly equal "ONE" and "THREE" beats. Since the rhythm is a little choppier than your average reel, the tempo slows down accordingly to keep from sounding sloppy: ♩ = 68 to ♩ = 80.

In some music books, you will find hornpipes written straight, with no dotted notes at all. In these instances, you just have to know that the tune is a hornpipe and should have a dotted feel. Actually, neither way of writing hornpipes is exactly correct. The dotted notes should not be held as long as they would be in classical music, but should easily swing. The best way to get the correct feel for hornpipes is to listen to recordings of them.

In American old-timey traditional playing, hornpipes and reels are often played almost the same, with similar tempos and straight rhythm. In your Irish settings, you will want to keep the two kinds of tunes clearly different.

**RHYTHMIC PRECISION**

When playing Irish dance tunes it is extremely important to keep your rhythm exactly on the money. Sure, this is tough. But since you are trying to play tunes designed around another instrument, you have to work a little harder to assure that the tune retains its Irish feeling.

Classical harp literature and even the classical-sounding Carolan tunes and other parlor pieces often favored by folk harpers have a way of letting the rhythm flow up and down in a dreamy fashion. But dance tunes can't be played dreamily and still sound like dance tunes. Getting the dances and dance tempos clearly in your head will help you develop your necessary internal metronome. And once the metronome is working, you are well on your way toward mastering the feel of Irish jigs, reels and hornpipes.

## TEMPOS

In the last few generations, as jigs and reels drifted farther and farther from their necessary connection with the dances, musicians have been more free to choose how fast to play them when dancers aren't present.

When playing dance tunes, it is extremely important to pick a tempo and stick to it throughout the piece. The dangers of rushing a tune are obvious -- not the least of which is that you won't be able to play the tune. Dragging the tempo can be just as annoying. Some phrases just sound sloppy and awkward when played too much slower than the original dance tempo. When playing with other musicians there is a common urge to play everything too fast. Medleys have a funny way of gradually speeding up, and long medleys can really get out of hand. Many musicians play as fast as their technique allows them to move their fingers. This is all good and exciting, but I feel the ideal speeds for these tunes are somewhat slower.

## MEDLEYS

There are uncounted ways to combine jigs and reels and hornpipes. Some are more common than others. First, tunes in the same key tend to go together rather easily. Also a tune in G major might go well into a tune in E minor, as the two keys are relative. Tension can be released in a medley by modulating up either a whole step, say from G to A, or up a fifth as from G to D, although, of course, this can be quite frustrating on the harp due to the necessary lever changes. Experimentation with different tune combinations can result in surprisingly satisfying transitions that you may not have heard other musicians try.

Using the tunes in this book, one common pairing of tunes is the *Earl's Chair* into *The Musical Priest* both of which are reels in B minor. The jig *The Blarney Pilgrim* goes nicely right into *Merrily Kiss the Quaker*. Slip-jigs are usually played with other slip-jigs, but that shouldn't prevent you from throwing *Rocky Road to Dublin* in with some plain old ordinary jigs.

Although less common, it is not unheard of to pair a jig with a reel or vice versa. So you can feel free to try setting up a fast reel with a slower jig, or a jig with a hornpipe, or any other combination that suits you. An easy-going version of *Off She Goes* could go into a steady, driving reel like *The Waterfall*, for instance.

Again, these are only a few suggestions. You will almost certainly chance upon some good combinations yourself. And experimentation is the only way to find them.

## PLAYING "FIDDLE TUNES" ON THE HARP

The harp, as you have probably gathered, is not as well suited to play fiddle tunes as a fiddle is. Nor is the harp historically the instrument first chosen to play these types of dance tunes. For centuries jigs and reels have been written for and played on fiddles, flutes, whistles, and various bagpipes, and more recently, even banjos, mandolins, and accordions. All these instruments have structural limitations which are quite different from those imposed on you by your harp. This means that ornaments or runs or arpeggios that are easy and comfortable on another instrument may be either uncomfortable or next to impossible for you. That is not something to worry about; it just means that a few compromises must be made.

Rather than trying to mimic a tenor banjo's fast triplets or the single-bow turns on the fiddle or a curiously indefinite note on the uilleann pipes, just work at hitting at the shape or feel of these ornaments. Or, sometimes more appropriate when playing with other musicians; simply leave space in your setting so whatever you do doesn't muddy up a phrase or ornament played by someone else. Sometimes hinting at a note or ornament can be just as effective as playing it. (See Sylvia's introduction for more on how to ornament pieces when playing solo.)

## WHAT IS AN IRISH MUSIC SESSION?

A lot of you have taken up the Celtic harp as a solitary instrument, because the sound delights you and the kind of music commonly played on a Celtic harp appeals to you somewhere deep down. But as much fun as it is to play the harp solo, it is equally pleasureable in a very different way to venture out and play with other instruments in sessions.

"What is a session?" I hear you cry. A session is a gathering of Irish or Scottish or other varied Celtic musicians, each wielding his or her choice of traditional instrument, and playing tunes as they pop into their heads or as they find tunes they know in common. Usually, sessions are dominated by lively dance tunes, including jigs and reels and hornpipes like those in this book. You will find sessions in pubs and bars and folk clubs and even in people's living-rooms, regularly scheduled or whenever the spirit moves them to play.

Sessions do not generally stipulate that one must be a flashy pro or possess a limitless repertoire in order to join in. And that's what makes them so much fun. Also, since the harp will often be drowned out by the other instruments, sessions provide a good opportunity for you to play without feeling like everyone is listening to you. By sitting in with many other musicians possessing various levels of expertise, you can quietly build up both your repertoire and your confidence about playing in public.

Listen before you play, but don't be shy. Feel free to play along with tunes you know. If you don't know the tune but can find the key, you might play chords in rhythm behind the others. The chordings provided for the tunes in this book give a good starting point for learning what chords fit what tunes. If you're unsure what chords are appropriate, you can always pedal along on the tonic (a D chord if the tune is in D). This has a similar effect to bagpipe drones in the ensemble and rarely sounds out of place, as long as you don't overdo it.

Like joining in any social setting that was there before you arrived, it helps to be polite. It is courteous to let different people start tunes and medleys from time to time. The role of tune starter is like the role of dealer in a card game. Everybody likes to be included. Since you play a relatively "unusual" and quiet instrument, you will generally not be a starter, but you'll probably find that they will ask you to play a "solo" from time to time as a change of pace. This is a great opportunity to perform airs, O'Carolan tunes, or other traditional pieces from your repertoire.

Another nice thing to do in sessions is to sit a tune out once in a while. When everybody plays all the time, the textures get dense and the sameness of the sound can get tiresome. If you sit out for a while, the ensemble will appreciate the sound of the harp all the more when you join back in.

## HOW ARE TUNES PLAYED IN SESSIONS?

There are many ways to play tunes and to string them together in sessions. There are, though, a few conventions that are common throughout most Irish sessions, and these help the beginning session participant know what to expect. First, most tunes are played at least twice all the way through, including all repeats.

Generally a tune isn't played more than four times or so before someone gets bored with it or thinks of another tune to medley into. This is a comforting thing to know if you are at a session collecting tunes by ear or by tape recorder. You generally have one pass through the tune to decide whether or not to turn on your recorder, or to listen for its shape and start to get a handle on how to pick it out by ear.

Another convention in sessions is that tunes are rarely played alone, but are instead strung together two or three or more in a row. After a while, in addition to listening to a tune as an individual entity, you will find yourself listening to how to get into it and out of it again. Whether a tune has a pickup or starts on the downbeat can determine what other tunes it can be matched up with easily.

Here's another quick note which harpers particularly have to keep in mind. As often as not, tunes get strung together because the fiddler or banjo player happened to think of it a split second before starting to play it. And so, from time to time you will find yourself suddenly not tuned to the key everyone else is furiously sawing away in. At the very least you'll be scrambling for your sharping levers, if you have them. But not to worry. You can either pedal along with appropriate drone notes or sit that one out and come in on the next tune.

## LEARNING TUNES BY EAR

Every musician picks up tunes at different rates of speed and with different degrees of sweating and cursing. Of course, there is no sure-fire easy way to learn a tune by ear. But here is one suggestion on how you might approach the problem. Start out by listening to the whole tune rather than the notes that make it up. Listen to the tune cycle all the way through and back to the beginning. Note whether it has two repeating parts (as most Irish dance tunes do), or if it has three or more. If you can tell what key it's in, fine, but don't worry about that right away. Instead, follow the rising and falling of the tune's phrases and arpeggios and scales before you start to plunk around on it. This is called listening for the shape of the tune.

In addition to being a good way to remember a tune more easily later, getting the shape of a tune clear in your head will help you recognize other settings of that tune, even if they are quite different. Every tune, you see, has dozens of settings, different because of geographic distance, or the limitations of the instruments, or the sheer perversity and ingenuity of the musician. But all settings will retain much the same shape and essence of the tune. So listen to see if a tune starts up high and dips down, or bubbles along in the middle, or changes keys in midstream. After that, learning it note for note can be much easier. You'll have a framework on which to place the notes. And you'll have a clearer idea of how to alter your version later without losing the essence of the tune.

# Blarney Pilgrim

arrangement by Sylvia Woods

Jig

# Garryowen

arrangement by Sylvia Woods

Jig

# Geese in the Bog

arrangement by Sylvia Woods

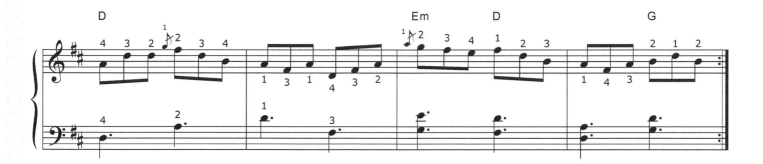

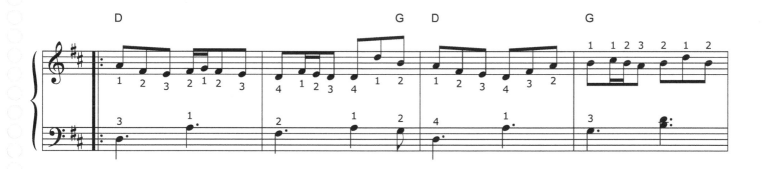

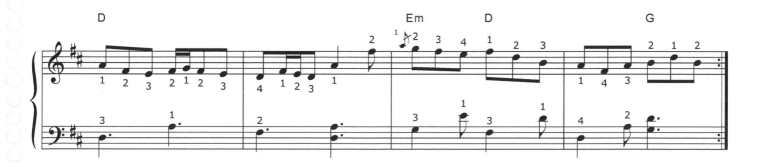

3

# Haste to the Wedding

arrangement by Sylvia Woods

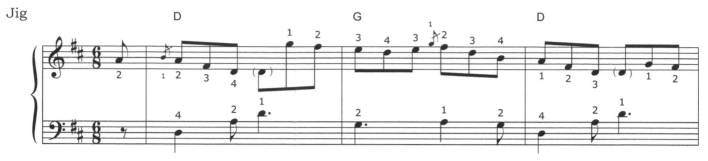

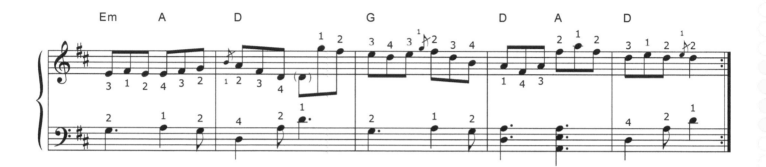

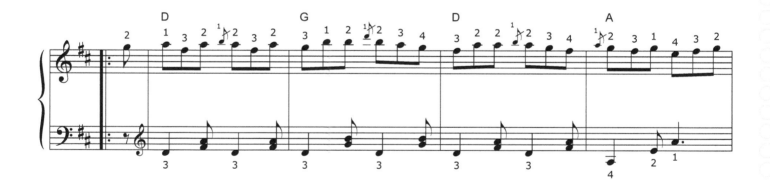

# Maid at the Spinning Wheel

## Hag at the Spinning Wheel

arrangement by Sylvia Woods

Jig

# Merrily Kiss the Quaker
## Merrily Kiss the Quaker's Wife

arrangement by Sylvia Woods

Jig

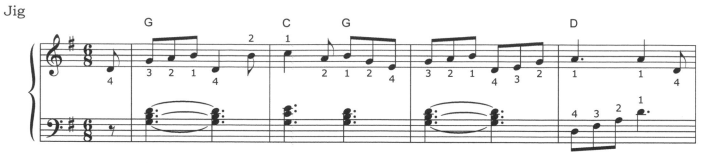

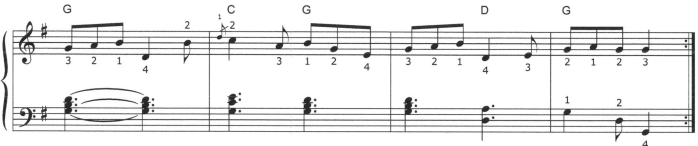

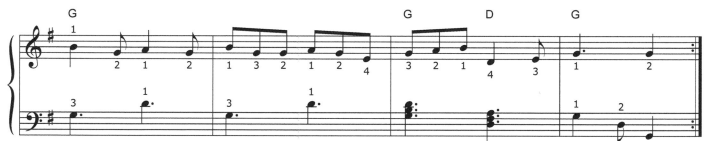

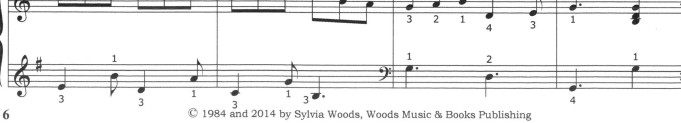

# Money in Both Pockets

arrangement by Sylvia Woods

Jig

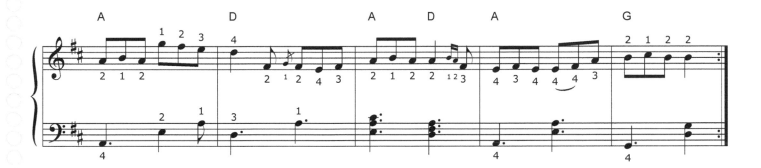

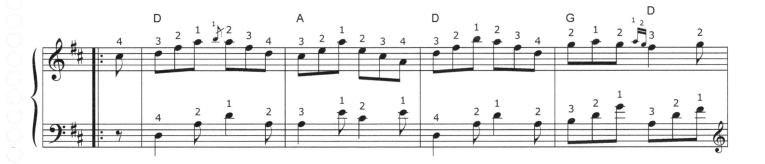

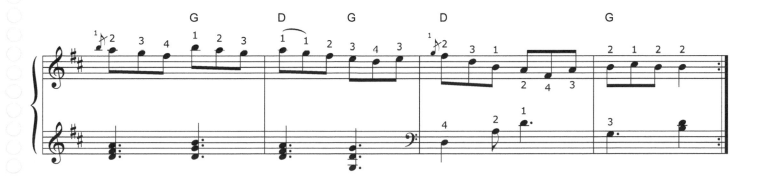

# Morrison's Jig

arrangement by Sylvia Woods

# Off She Goes

arrangement by Sylvia Woods

Jig

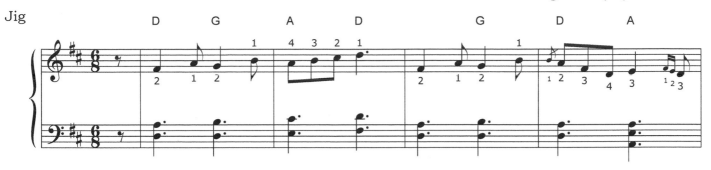

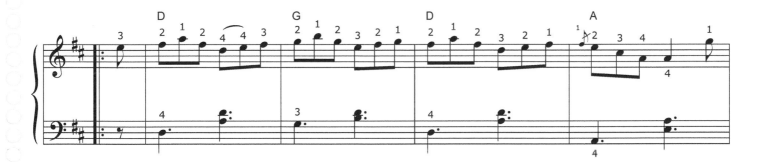

9

# Road to Lisdoonvarna

arrangement by Sylvia Woods

Jig

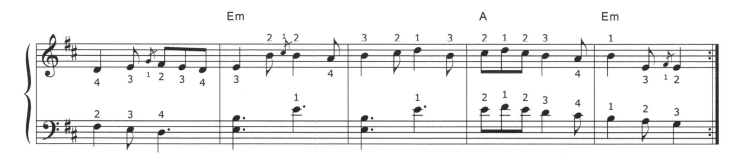

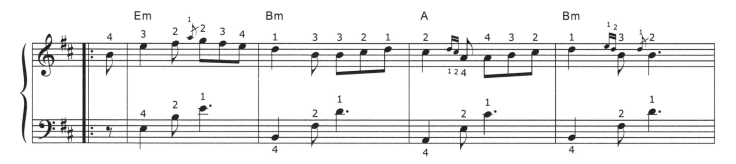

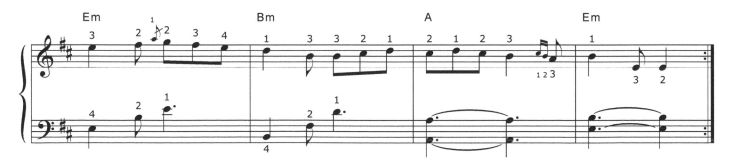

# Smash the Windows

### Roaring Jelly

arrangement by Sylvia Woods

Jig

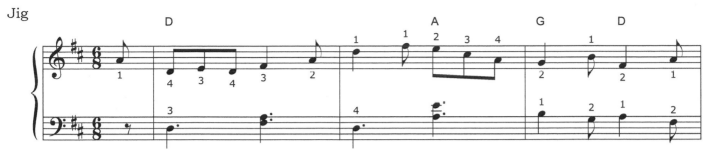

**11**

# Tobin's Favorite

arrangement by Sylvia Woods

Jig

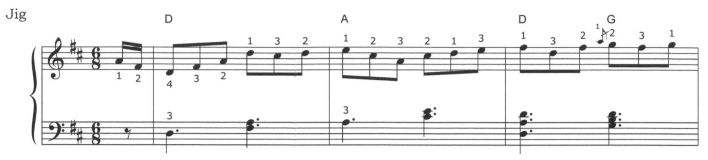

# A Fig for a Kiss
## Milk the Churn OR Two in a Gig

arrangement by Sylvia Woods

Slip Jig

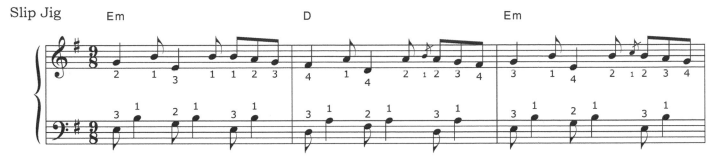

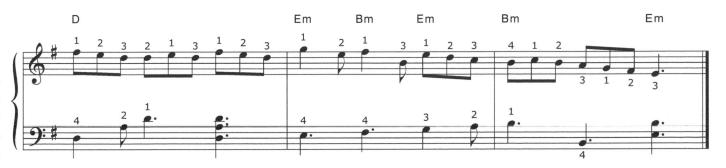

**13**

# Boys of Ballysodare

arrangement by Sylvia Woods

Slip Jig

# Dublin Streets

arrangement by Sylvia Woods

Slip Jig

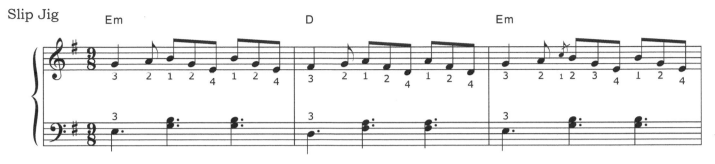

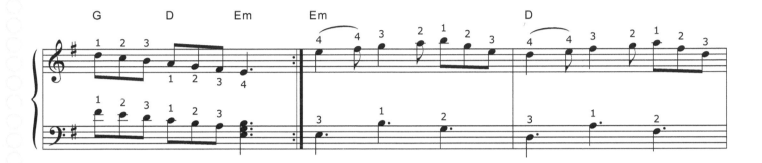

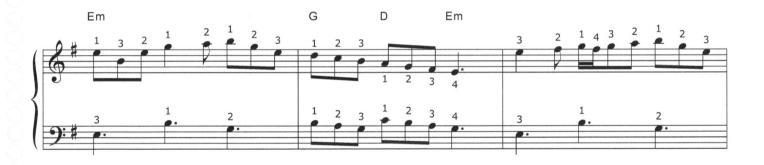

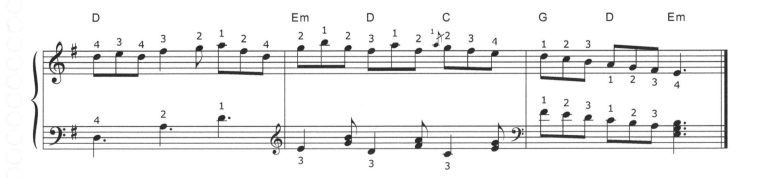

# Give Us a Drink of Water

arrangement by Sylvia Woods

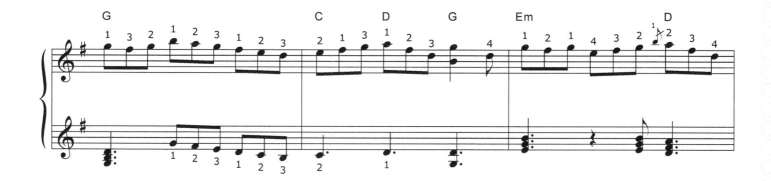

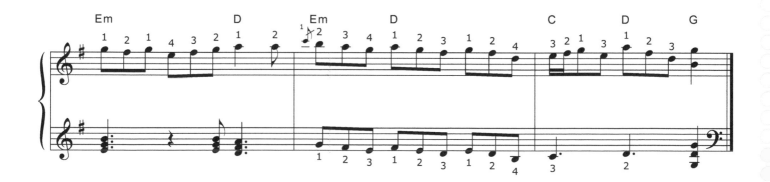

# Hardiman the Fiddler

arrangement by Sylvia Woods

Slip Jig

# Kid on the Mountain

arrangement by Sylvia Woods

Slip Jig

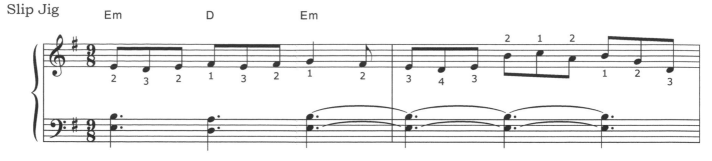

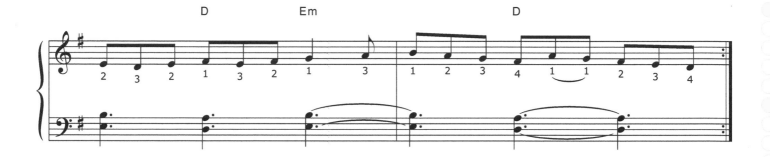

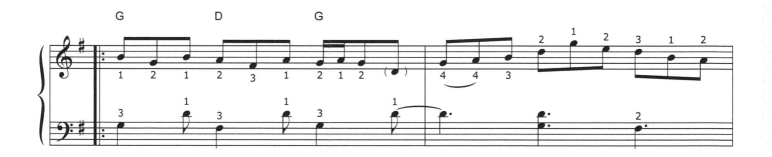

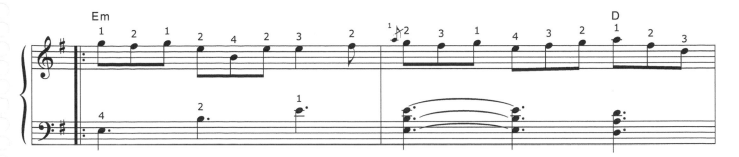

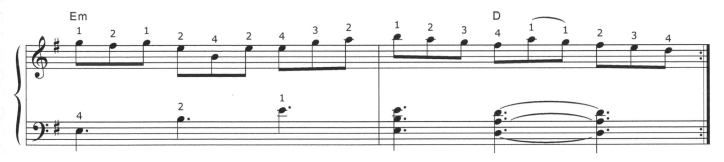

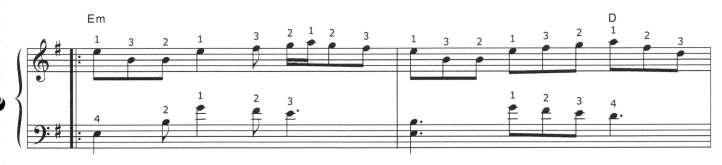

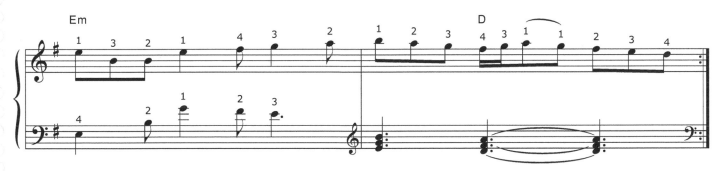

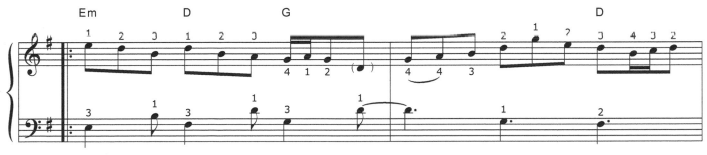

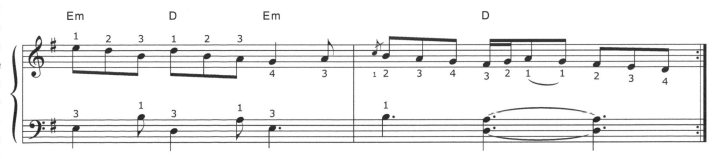

# Rocky Road to Dublin

arrangement by Sylvia Woods

# Boys of Blue Hill

arrangement by Sylvia Woods

Hornpipe

# Fisher's Hornpipe
## Fisherman's Hornpipe

arrangement by Sylvia Woods

Hornpipe

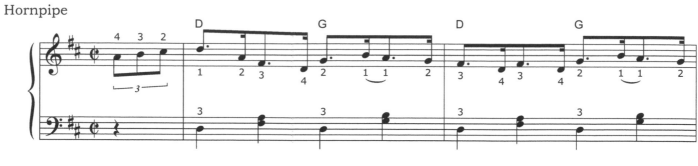

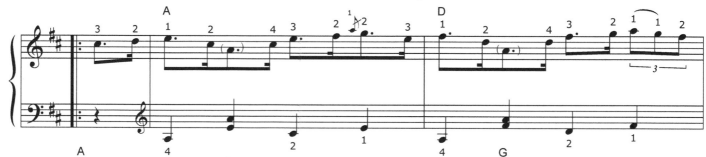

# Ladies' Hornpipe

arrangement by Sylvia Woods

Hornpipe

# Little Beggarman
## Redhaired Boy

arrangement by Sylvia Woods

Hornpipe

© 1984 and 2014 by Sylvia Woods, Woods Music & Books Publishing

# O'Donnell's Hornpipe

arrangement by Sylvia Woods

Hornpipe

25

# Off to California

arrangement by Sylvia Woods

Hornpipe

# Plains of Boyle

arrangement by Sylvia Woods

Hornpipe

# Rights of Man

arrangement by Sylvia Woods

Hornpipe

* The C# can be kept through the repeat, but must be natural the 2nd time through if you are going back to the beginning.

# Soldier's Joy

arrangement by Sylvia Woods

Hornpipe

**29**

# Earl's Chair

arrangement by Sylvia Woods

Reel

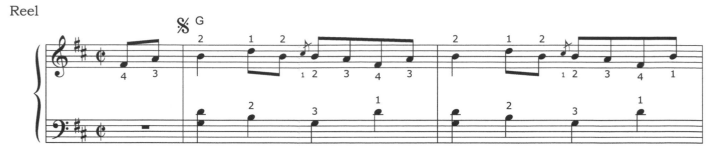

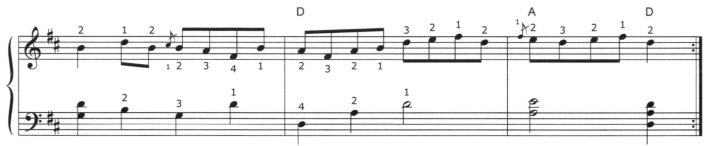

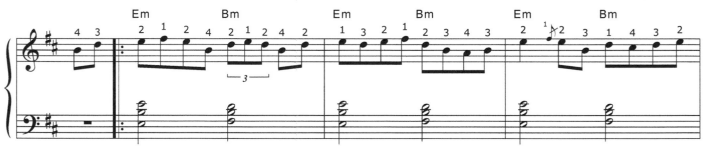

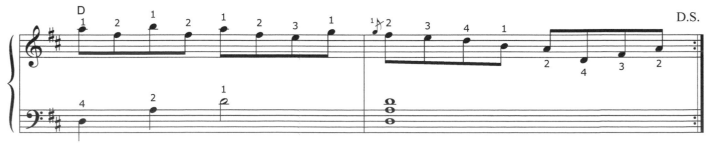

# Fairy Dance Reel
# Fairy Reel

arrangement by Sylvia Woods

# Green Fields of America

*arrangement by Sylvia Woods*

# Leather Buttons

arrangement by Sylvia Woods

# Maid Behind the Bar

arrangement by Sylvia Woods

Reel

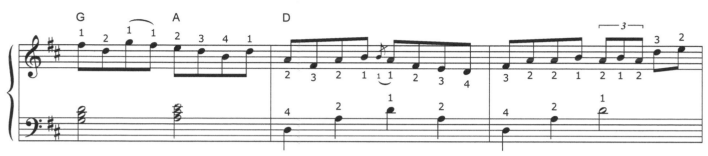

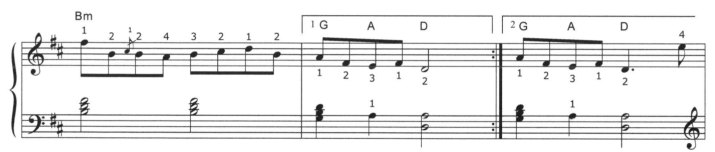

34

# Mason's Apron

arrangement by Sylvia Woods

# Miss McLeod's Reel

arrangement by Sylvia Woods

# Music in the Glen

arrangement by Sylvia Woods

Reel

37

# Musical Priest

arrangement by Sylvia Woods

Reel

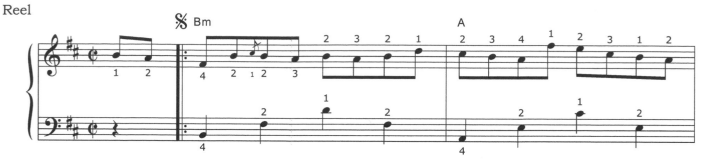

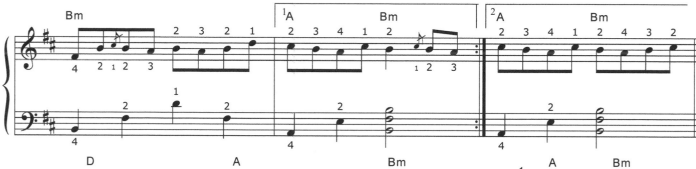

# Tent at the Fair

arrangement by Sylvia Woods

Reel

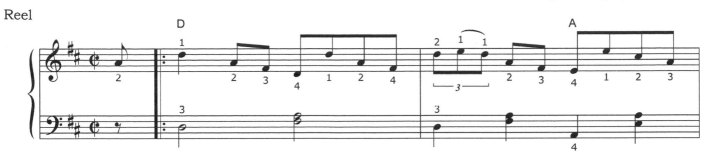

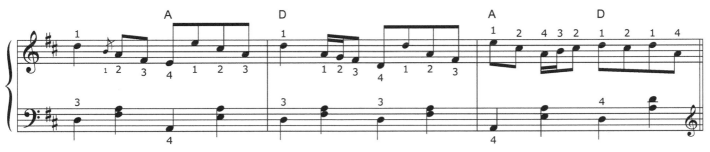

# Thro' the Field
# Miss Thornton's Reel

arrangement by Sylvia Woods

Reel

# The Waterfall

arrangement by Sylvia Woods

# Who Made Your Breeches?

arrangement by Sylvia Woods

**Reel**

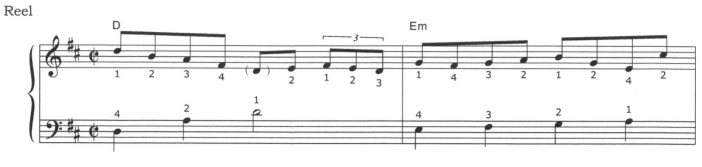

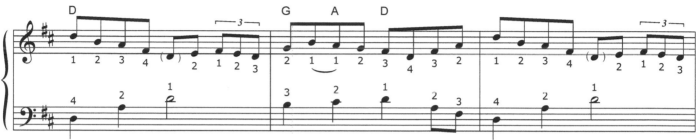

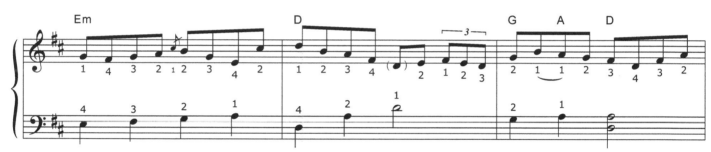

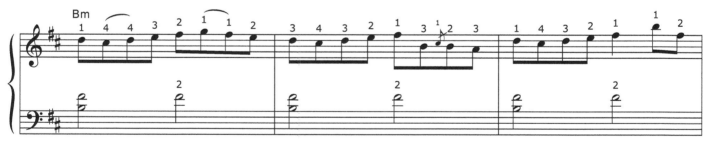

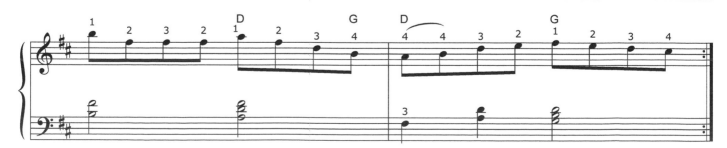

# The Wind that Shakes the Barley

arrangement by Sylvia Woods

43

# The Wise Maid

Collected from John Doherty, Donegal fiddle player
Reel

arrangement by Sylvia Woods

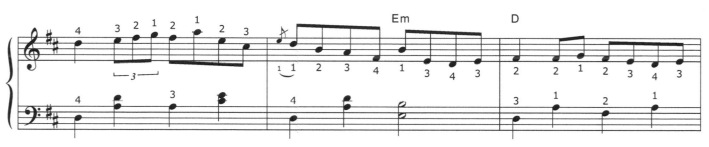

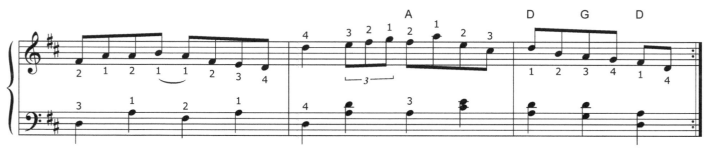

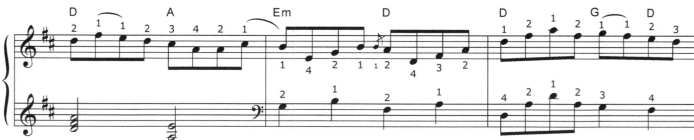

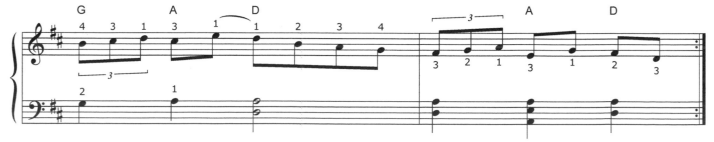

# The Battle of Aughrim

arrangement by Sylvia Woods

March

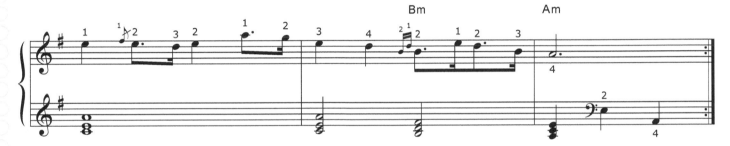

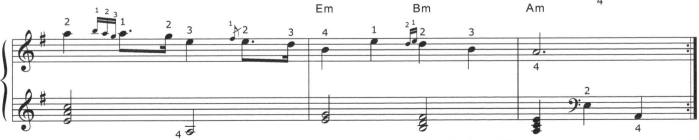

# Brian Boru's March

arrangement by Sylvia Woods

46

# Pig-Town Fling

arrangement by Sylvia Woods

Fling

# Carrickfergus

arrangement by Sylvia Woods

Air

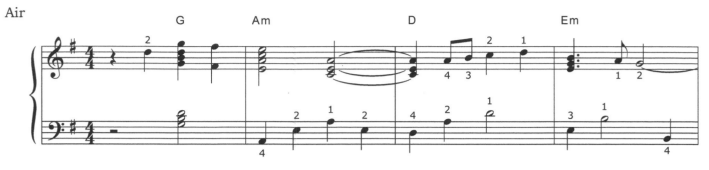

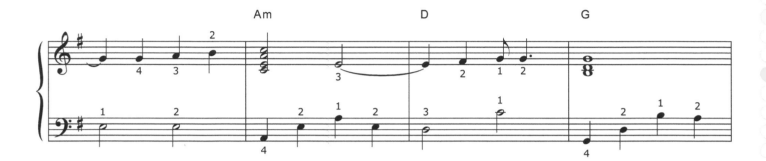

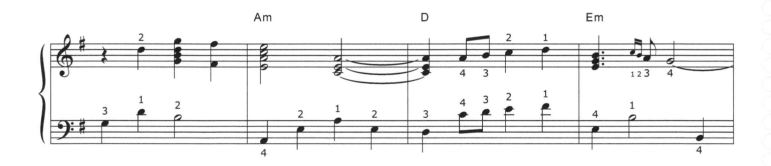

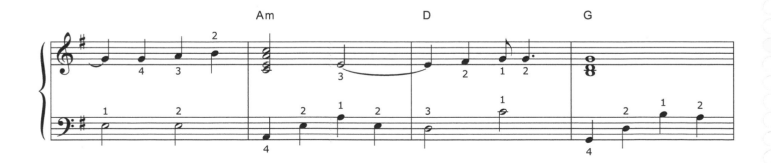

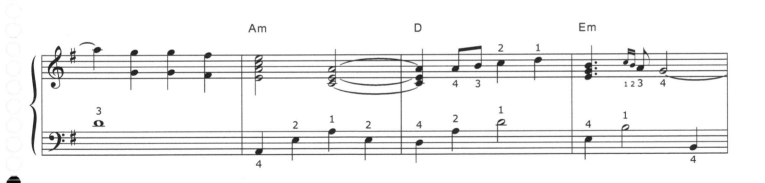

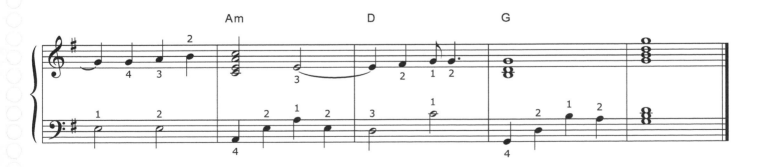

# King of the Fairies

arrangement by Sylvia Woods

Set Dance

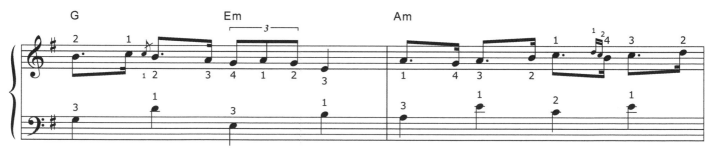

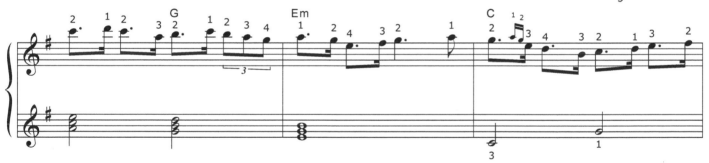

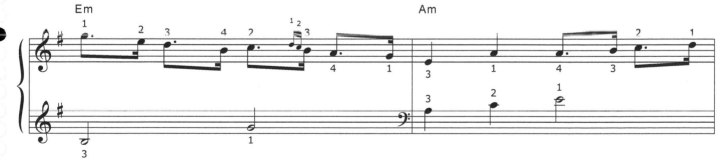

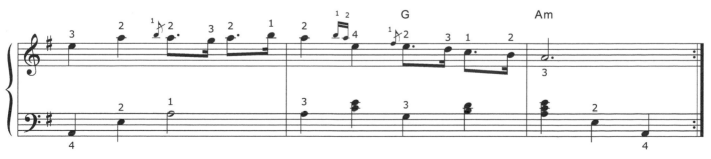

# March of the King of Laois

arrangement by Sylvia Woods

March

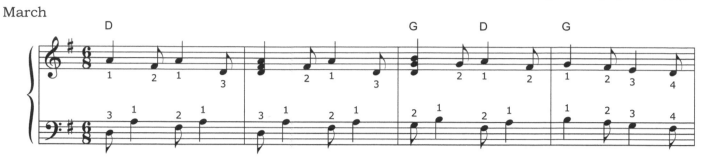

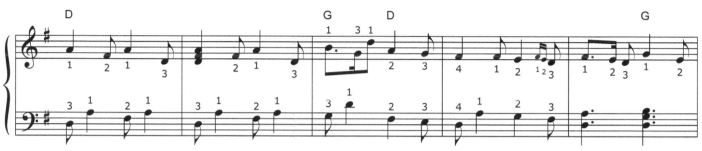

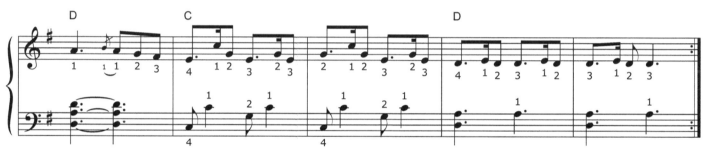

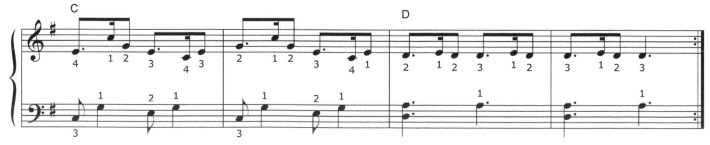

# The Parting Glass

arrangement by Sylvia Woods

Air

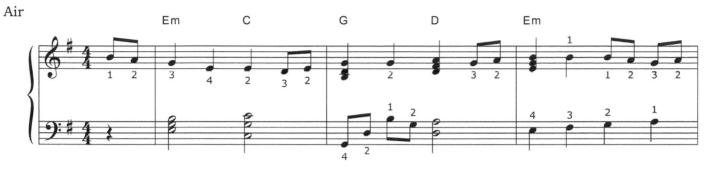

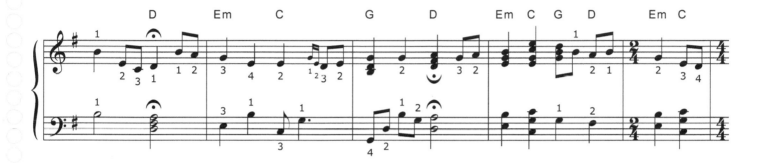

# More Harp Books of Celtic Music by Sylvia Woods

These three books are part of the Sylvia Woods Multi-Level Harp Book Series: books designed to be used by harp players at all levels of proficiency. Each of the pieces has two arrangements: an easy version, and one that is more difficult. The two arrangements can be played together as a duet. Each piece includes chord notations that can be used by harpers or other instrumentalists. Fingerings are included.

Companion CDs are also available for these books as well as the Irish Dance Tunes book that you are currently reading. Sylvia plays the pieces slower than usual, so you can play along while you're learning.

The books are also available in a PDF download format, and the CDs as mp3s at www.harpcenter.com.

### 50 Irish Melodies for the Harp

Here are 50 of your favorite Irish songs (with lyrics) in multi-level arrangements for harp by Sylvia Woods. As well as songs from Ireland, this book also includes some Irish-American songs that have found their way into the Irish music tradition, such as *When Irish Eyes Are Smiling, Too-Ra-Loo-Ra-Loo-Ral,* and *My Wild Irish Rose.* This book will be invaluable on St. Patrick's Day, but is fun all year 'round! All the pieces are fingered and are in the key of C or sharp keys. Lyrics and chord symbols are indicated. Some require lever or pedal changes within the piece. 112 pages, spiral-bound. *Contents: Avenging and Bright; Believe Me If All Those Endearing Young Charms; Bendemeer's Stream; Castle of Dromore; Cockles and Mussels; The Cruiskeen Lawn; Danny Boy; Dear Little Shamrock; Down by the Salley Gardens; Famine Song; Fanaid Grove; Farewell! But Whenever You Welcome the Hour; Farewell to Liverpool; Flight of the Earls; Foggy Dew; Galway Piper; Gartan Mother's Lullaby; Gentle Maiden; The Girl I Left Behind Me; Good Night; Has Sorrow Thy Young Days Shaded?; I Know My Love; Kathleen Mavourneen; Kerry Dance; Killarney; Lark in the Clear Air; Lark in the Morning; The Leprechaun; Limerick is Beautiful; Mairi's Wedding; My Lagan Love; My Wild Irish Rose; My Yellow-Haired Lad; O'Donnell Aboo; Ould Plaid Shawl; Over the Hills and Far Away; Rakes of Mallow; Rose of Tralee; Rosin The Bow; Saint Patrick's Day; She Moved Through the Fair; Shule Aroon; Snowy-Breasted Pearl; Spanish Lady; Spinning Wheel Song; Sweet Carnloch Bay; Sweet Rosie O'Grady; 'Tis the Last Rose of Summer; Too-Ra-Loo-Ra-Loo-Ral; Wearin' O' the Green; When Irish Eyes Are Smiling.*

### 40 O'Carolan Tunes for All Harps

O'Carolan (sometimes called Carolan) was one of the best-known of the Irish harpers. He lived from 1670-1738. After being blinded by smallpox in his teens, he learned to play the harp. For the rest of his years he traveled throughout Ireland as an itinerant musician. His compositions are popular with harp players as well as other Irish musicians. This multi-level book by Sylvia Woods contains 40 tunes by O'Carolan. They are perfect for weddings and other occasions. All pieces are fingered and are in the key of C or sharp keys. 112 pages, spiral-bound. *Contents: Lady Athenry; George Brabazon; Planxty Burke; Carolan's Cap; Carolan's Concerto (Mrs. Power); Carolan's Draught; Carolan's Fancy; Carolan's Farewell to Music; Carolan's Quarrel with the Landlady; Carolan's Receipt; Carolan's Welcome; The Clergy's Lamentation; Sir Charles Coote; Planxty Crilly; Bridget Cruise; Planxty Drew; John Drury; Lord Galway's Lamentation; Lady Gethin; Hewlett; Lord Inchiquin; Baptist Johnston; Bumper Squire Jones (Thomas Morres Jones); Morgan Magan; Blind Mary; Mrs. Maxwell; John O'Connor; Maurice O'Connor; Charles O'Conor; Hugh O'Donnell; O'Flinn; Kean O'Hara; O'Rourke's Feast; Eleanor Plunkett; Fanny Power; Planxty Safaigh; Sheebeg and Sheemore; Dr. John Stafford; Captain Sudley (Carolan's Dowry); Planxty Sweeny.*

### 52 Scottish Tunes for All Harps

This book includes 52 of your favorite Scottish songs (with lyrics) in multi-level arrangements for harp. Over half are by Robert Burns. Each piece has two arrangements: an easy version, and one that is more difficult. The pieces are fingered and in the key of C or sharp keys, and chord symbols are indicated. A few require lever or pedal changes. 112 pages, spiral-bound. *Contents: Annie Laurie; Auld Lang Syne; Ay Waukin O; Baloo Baleerie; The Birks of Aberfeldy; The Blue Bells of Scotland; The Boatie Rows; Bonnie Bell; Bonnie Dundee; Bonnie Wee Thing; Braw Braw Lads; Buy Broom Besoms; Ca' the Yowes To the Knowes; Charlie Is My Darling; Comin' Thro' The Rye; Corn Rigs Are Bonnie; Dumbarton's Drums; Duncan Gray; Flow Gently Sweet Afton; The Flowers O' the Forest; Green Grow the Rashes O!; Hame, Hame, Hame; Ho Ro My Nut-Brown Maiden; Hieland Laddie; I Aince Lo'ed a Lass; I'll Ay Ca' In by Yon Toun; Jock O'Hazeldean; John Anderson My Jo; The Keel Row; Kelvin Grove; Land O' the Leal; Lassie Wi' the Lint-White Locks; The Lea Rig; Leezie Lindsay; Loch Lomond; Loch Tay Boat Song; A Man's a Man for A' That; My Heart's In the Highlands; My Love is Like a Red Red Rose; My Love She's But a Lassie Yet; My Nanie O; Rantin' Rovin' Robin; Rattlin' Roarin' Willie; A Rosebud by My Early Walk; The Rowan Tree; Scotland the Brave; Scots Wha Hae; Skye Boat Song Wae's Me for Prince Charlie; The White Cockade; Will Ye No Come Back Again?; Ye Banks and Braes.*

# Additional Harp Music by Sylvia Woods

## SHEET MUSIC

*All of Me*
*All the Pretty Little Horses*
*America Medley*
Music from Disney-Pixar's <u>Brave</u>
*Bring Him Home* from <u>Les Misérables</u>
*Castle on a Cloud* from <u>Les Misérables</u>
Music from <u>A Charlie Brown Christmas</u>
*Dead Poets Society*
*Fields of Gold*
*Fireflies*
*Flower Duet*
Music from Disney's <u>Frozen</u>
*Harpers are Not Bizarre*
*House at Pooh Corner*
*In the Bleak Midwinter*
*Into the West* from <u>Lord of the Rings</u>
*Mary Did You Know?*
Mendelssohn's *Wedding March*
*My Heart Will Go On* from <u>Titanic</u>
*Over the Rainbow* from <u>Wizard of Oz</u>
*River Flows in You*
*Safe & Sound*
*Say Something*
*Simple Gifts*
*Spiritual Medley*
*Stairway to Heaven*
Music from Disney's <u>Tangled</u>
*A Thousand Years*
*The Water is Wide*
*Winter Bells*
*Wondrous Love*
Theme from Disney-Pixar's <u>Up</u>

## BOOKS

*Beauty and the Beast*
*Chanukah Music*
*50 Christmas Carols*
*John Denver Love Songs*
*76 Disney Songs*
*Gecko Tails*
*Groovy Songs of the 60s*
*The Harp of Brandiswhiere*
*Four Holiday Favorites*
*Hymns and Wedding Music*
*50 Irish Melodies*
*Jesu, Joy of Man's Desiring*
*Lennon and McCartney*
*Music Theory & Arranging Techniques*
*40 O'Carolan Tunes*
*Pachelbel's Canon*
*22 Romantic Songs*
*52 Scottish Songs*
*Teach Yourself to Play the Folk Harp*
*Andrew Lloyd Webber Music*
*The Wizard of Oz*

---

Available from your local harp store or from
Sylvia Woods Harp Center
PO Box 223434, Princeville, Hawaii 96722 USA
www.harpcenter.com

# ALPHABETICAL INDEX OF TUNES

A Fig for a Kiss................13

Battle of Aughrim.................45

Blarney Pilgrim......................1

Boys of Ballysodare.................14

Boys of Blue Hill.................21

Brian Boru's March .................46

Carrickfergus.................48

Dublin Streets .................15

Earl's Chair .................30

Fairy Dance Reel .................31

Fairy Reel .................31

Fisher's Hornpipe .................22

Fisherman's Hornpipe.................22

Garryowen.................2

Geese in the Bog.................3

Give Us a Drink of Water.................16

Green Fields of America.................32

Hag at the Spinning Wheel.................5

Hardiman the Fiddler.................17

Haste to the Wedding.................4

Kid on the Mountain.................18

King of the Fairies .................50

Ladies' Hornpipe.................23

Leather Buttons.................33

Little Beggarman .................24

Maid at the Spinning Wheel.................5

Maid Behind the Bar.................34

March of the King of Laois .................52

Mason's Apron.................35

Merrily Kiss the Quaker .................6

Merrily Kiss the Quaker's Wife.................6

Milk the Churn.................13

Miss McLeod's Reel.................36

Miss Thornton's Reel.................40

Money in Both Pockets.................7

Morrison's Jig.................8

Music in the Glen.................37

Musical Priest .................38

O'Donnell's Hornpipe.................25

Off She Goes.................9

Off to California .................26

Parting Glass.................53

Pig Town Fling.................47

Plains of Boyle.................27

Redhaired Boy .................24

Rights of Man .................28

Road to Lisdoonvarna.................10

Roaring Jelly .................11

Rocky Road to Dublin .................20

Smash the Windows.................11

Soldier's Joy .................29

Tent at the Fair.................39

Thro' the Field.................40

Tobin's Favorites.................12

Two in a Gig .................13

Waterfall.................41

Who Made Your Breeches? .................42

Wind that Shakes the Barley .................43

Wise Maid.................44